To Felicia

Be Blessed

S.T.Y.L.E.

On The

Inside

By

Deborah R. Houston

"Debb"

Printed in the United States of America

First Printing: June 2016

ISBN-978-0692205877

TABLE OF CONTENTS

This book is dedicated to those whom I have given my life-force, my daughters, Amber and Janae.

Being chosen by God to be your mother is my greatest joy and I am forever humbled to be blessed with such a rewarding responsibility.

As you mature, and as I grow older, I find that you have taught me so much about life. I appreciate your fun-loving spirit, your gifts and talents and most of all, your love for our God.

It is my prayer that as you continue to grow, that you will walk in your God-breathed purpose with STYLE.

Love Always,

Mom

PREFACE

Everyone wants to be fashionably correct, tastefully dressed, and even red carpet ready.

Everyone wants to be in STYLE.

If you want to turn heads, stand up and be noticed and bring the board room to a standstill upon your entrance, it doesn't start with being in style, but rather embracing and empowering the woman within, therefore, focusing on your S.T.Y.L.E. On The Inside.

S.T.Y.L.E. On the Inside reminds you and teaches you the importance of adorning your inner being. The result is the dazzling shimmer and shine of your outer woman.

Within these pages are five life-changing principles that will positively impact you and take you to another level of being your best self, while encouraging others to do the same.

The journey begins to your S.T.Y.L.E. On The Inside.

Debb Houston

"I will praise Thee;
for I am fearfully and wonderfully made:"

~Psalm 139:14a~

"Fashion is fleeting,

STYLE is eternal."

~Yves Saint Laurent~

STYLE ON THE INSIDE

Every day, women are informed of what the world and society considers as fashionably and stylishly acceptable.

We constantly witness the airing of commercials, advertisements, reality television shows, talk shows and various magazines that offer advice on how an individual can become more successful. We are constantly schooled on ways to demand and receive respect and even change the game in any boardroom by being told that our success is linked to our attire.

With every awards show, as celebrities showcase their designer duds down the red carpet, with cameras flashing like fireworks and reporters jockeying for interview positions, usually the first question to be asked beyond the usual pleasantries is, 'Who are you wearing today?' The answer is usually a famous or up and coming designer, whose name floats into the atmosphere. These celebrities are picked apart from their hairstyles, jewelry choices, colors chosen, gowns or tuxes worn, shoes worn, make up chosen and even the upswept design of hair in order to inform us of what is considered to be posh, chic and fabulously fashionable.

It would appear that while celebrities stroll, strut and step along the red carpet, a much less famous designer, somewhere, feverishly begins to cut, layout and sew a pattern in order to duplicate the hottest gown, dress or even tux at a fraction of the cost for the average consumer. By the next morning, their less expensive creation is paraded on various morning shows, in hopes, that women or men will take note and take action in order to purchase the knock-off design, therefore making its' wearer in style.

By the end of the day, fashion experts share their opinion of the hits or misses, queens or flubs, and kings or killers of fashion and even whether or not celebrities have shown us how to be subtle, safe or stunning.

However, to be in style goes beyond attire, for fashionably correct choices are even given for our homes by way of the shape and size of living, dining and bedroom furniture, wall colors or even the hottest shades to bring out the best look for your kitchen.

Time and time again, we are told that we can rule while wearing stilettos, gain power while adorned in a skirt or even climb and eventually control the corporate ladder with the bangles, bracelets and bling. And after conquering all throughout the course of our day, we can go to a home fit for the portrayal of success that we strive to attain.

It's all about your style. Your one-of-a-kind way of doing what you do. The swerve of your sashay, the switch of your hips, the single or double-knot of your scarf, length of your coiffed hair, twist of dreads, lace of tennis shoes or wedges, fit and flow of the material, color and shade, and even the funk and fabric. It's all about the style. Who's in and who's out. Who's hot and who's not.

However, your style is an exhibition and an excursion of more than 'who you're wearing' or 'what you're wearing', it's much deeper and broader than the style on the outside, for what you do, what you wear, where you go, how you roll and what you say is all about your style on the inside.

As it is true that as a woman, we can rule while wearing our stilettos and yes, we are beyond capable of standing at the top of any corporate ladder, it all begins with adorning the woman within. It's all about your STYLE ~ On The Inside. When what you think of yourself and what you know of yourself are fully embraced and fully accepted, it speaks volumes and is made manifest through your outward appearance in the advertisement and portrayal of you.

STYLE ON THE

INSIDE

'S'

STRENGTH TO STRUT

Strength:

The authority and ownership of

greater than average power

Strut:

To display one's best work

The behind-the-scenes energy was through the roof. The electricity in the air bounced from person to person, using them as transformers ready to explode. The bass vibrated throughout the entire room full of chairs that lined the outer edges of the stage and rolled over from row to row to row. People mingled, rubbed elbows, clinked their glasses together and waited for the show to begin, the runway show.

My heart was beating in time with the rhythm of the bass while my nerves were on edge. It was my first runway show. I had already gone to the first station, where my flawless make-up had been professionally applied by a Caucasian woman who told me that she was, 'indeed the black man', as a means of confirming her sexual preference and her love for African-Americans. I had just sat down in a directors' type of chair at the hair station where the stylist looked me over, asked about my outfits for the runway show and proceeded to pull, brush, comb, and apply enough spritz to my hair until he achieved his desired look, a straight and pulled back look in order to highlight what he referred to as 'Asian features'.

As I moved out of the chair for the next model to be primped, I walked over to my station where my outfits were hanging, unbuttoned or unzipped, and shoes were unfastened or untied, all ready for wear.

The room was abuzz with bodies moving, constant chatter and the energy was as high as the ceiling. The scents of various hair products and sprays floated above, giving the room a hazy glow. This very room could be ground zero for the hole that was created in the ozone layer.

The drink and snack station were set up in the corner that consisted of various types of cubed cheeses, salamis, dips, crackers, raw veggies, fruit, and enough top shelf liquor to drown away any sorrow. I was amazed that they would even supply food for women and men who prided themselves on being as waif thin as possible, to the extent that some would consider one cube of that cheese as their only meal for the day. That, perhaps, explained its' no man's land existence, save the potbelly, hungry eyed security guard. My mind told me that he was licking his lips in hopes of human consumption more so than the trays of provided food.

Here in the midst of it all, I stood watching and listening. Some models moved from station to station, others chatted about the work they'd done, another gazed into mirrors while silently taking a quick and sizing glance at others. All were hoping that the show would go well for them. I silently evaluated myself among my company of those who had been there and done that. As I looked over the expensive clothing that I was about to showcase in front of hundreds of people, my fears crept to the forefront of my mind. What if I tripped? Lord, what if I fell? What if some reporter or magazine columnist talked about my being the worst representation of a model they had ever seen?

My condemning thoughts were interrupted by the runway show organizers time call, informing all models that we needed to be dressed and in our first outfit, for the show was about to begin. As I quickly dressed, being careful not to ruin the work of the makeup artist and the hair stylist, my mind shifted to the long runway that was waiting for me around the wall of curtains. As all of the models found their place in line, I took my own, as we inched closer and closer to the parted curtain. The assistant show coordinator, wearing an an earphone in one ear and a lapel mic, would give us a quick look over before nodding her affirmation for us to grace the catwalk. I hoped it would be nothing more than a simple stroll in the park, though I knew it meant much more.

Perhaps the organizer sensed my nervousness. It could be that my body language betrayed me. I don't know. What I do know is that as my right foot, my dominant lead foot, took me closer to the curtain, the assistant coordinator gently placed her hand on my shoulder, grabbing my attention and looking into my eyes. For a split second, it was as if the bass and music had stopped playing, and all that I could hear were her words, that catapulted me into another realm of consciousness as she told me, "You got this!" It was at that very moment that I realized that I was ready and that I possessed the power and the strength to strut, and that I did.

You're stronger than you think!

You didn't think that you had what it takes to make it – but you did!

You couldn't even see yourself being here today – but you are!

There were times when you felt as if it was all over for you - but it wasn't!

You're stronger than what they said!
The thought of you, that started in someone's feeble mind, flowed through their lips and was shared with another, was only based on their personal issues and perceptions about life. No one else can even begin to touch the depth of who you are and the strength that you possess. It doesn't matter what he or she said. It's not about who or what has entered your atmosphere because when it gets right down to it, what really matters is you - your perception of you. For someone else to say that you are less than another or that you're not worth anything will only become a reality if you choose to embrace what has been said and act upon that belief. If you are told that you are more than what you have

become and that you have what it takes to reach the stars, yet you have already bought into a penny candy or dollar store mentality of your worth, you are, therefore, unable to grasp your beyond-worthiness. Who you are, your ability, your power and your strength starts and ends with you.

You're stronger than what you're dealing with right now. Life came along, rather unexpectedly, and dealt an uppercut for which you weren't prepared. Had warning been given, chances are, you might have tried to avoid what has now surrounded you. Yet, even during those times when proper planning and procedures have been followed, life still has a way of surprising you and catching you off guard. The manner in which life approaches and makes its' appearance is not what matters for the happenings of it are oftentimes beyond your control. What matters most is your reaction to what has transpired and I'm here to remind you that no matter who or what it is, no matter how its' packaged, regardless of the height, depth and scope of it, you, are stronger than what has entered your atmosphere. You are a who, not a what.

You possess a power and a strength that exceeds anything that you will ever encounter, so much so, that after the 'it' and the 'what' have vacated your atmosphere, the presence of your power will not only give you the strength to stand, but to begin to strut.

Based on your existence and your ability to outwalk, outrun and outlast whatever or whoever made it their business to hinder and handcuff you, today, you have the authoritative right and the strength to strut. You can rise above the mediocrity of simply living. You can ascend above the standards that were set by someone else that never took the time to even know your name. You can step above and beyond the boundaries that were set for you – by you. For those boundaries were built on fear. The line that you dared yourself to cross, you thought that it would serve as your end, when in reality, it served as the starting point for your race of destiny in order to begin your strut.

A strut, in the fashion industry, calls for one to walk, saunter, march, and take steps of confidence that will demand attention. To do so leaves others in a state of awe and wonderment in the wake of the individual's absence. Prior to my entrance onto the catwalk, the words 'You've got this' spoken from the assistant director, told me that my walk or my strut down that runway would inform all onlookers that I was taking ownership of myself and the outfit that was chosen for me. However, to strut is much deeper than what is portrayed on any runway. For every woman, be it a fashion model, teacher, baker, doctor, domestic engineer, and all walks of like, to strut encompasses the ability of being true to who you are, owning who you are and sharing who you are with the world. Not as a means of showmanship, but servitude. It is the confidence of what you've been given and the commitment to use it for the betterment of your world and those around you. As you strut, you are authorizing the power that you possess and you are also owning your testimony of the strength that was required for you to arrive at this point in your life.

The strength to strut grants permission for others to do the same. It encourages you to share the blessing of the gift and talent that you have been given while reminding others that they, too, possess something that was given solely to them to make this world a better place.

So, what does it mean to strut? Whatever your definition, it must be molded to mesh with the identity of who you are, not who you claim to be, for the two can be at opposite ends of the spectrum. Many times, we offer a false snapshot of ourselves based on how we would like to be accepted in a society that urges us to conform to a style that comes and goes with the rushing tide. Yet to offer the world the totality of who you are, in your natural glory or to take steps to do so, which will lead to your strut, takes courage and determination.

So, again, what does it mean to strut? To strut is your walk, your swagger, the fluid movement and motion of the woman that you are. It's the ability to march to the beat of your drum. It's calls for you be in time, in tune and to trust in the natural God-created, God-inspired and God-given totality of who you are. When you are seen and looked upon and even during your encounters, men and women cannot help but to take note and nod with approval and admiration.

If you are one who has accepted, given birth to the truth of who you are, and are willing to step in time with the strut that was designed solely for you, your timely and timeless walk may be greeted by the green eyed monster of jealousy, but you are not discouraged, phased nor deterred.

Your strut lends a light to those unwilling to recognize their own and to light a path to those seeking the rhythm of their inner metronome. To strut is a step of confidence. It is a walk of assuredness because you know where you've been and you've learned the life lesson that was taught. You're aware of where it is you're striving to go and despite the hurdles that were placed to impede your progress, while you strut, you possess an unwavering determination and strength to keep the pace in order to meet your desired goals.

Your strut are the steps toward the wholeness and completion of who you were meant to be.

Your strut refuses to take faulty steps of uncertainty, for you're walking by faith, even into the unknown glory of the destiny that awaits you.

And so…you have the strength to strut!!! You strut with a glide of giftedness. You walk with your head held high, your shoulders pushed back, your arms swinging by your side, with a smile that speaks of the grace you've received and a gleam of glory in your eyes. You strut!!!

Sometimes your strut demands a stomp. Not one of anger but a stomp that informs the world that you will not be a co-signer of wrong doing nor a sideliner of negativity. Other days your strut requires that you dance the night away with a celebratory rhythm and rhyme to the bass, melody or funk that surrounds your moment to trip the light fantastic, causing you to shimmy, sway, two-step, boogie, rock, roll, twist, shuffle or even jitterbug.

Your strut, your walk, your gait, your march, your stroll, your saunter is a parade of you and yourself. You are the band leader, percussion, woodwind and brass sections all rolled up into one. You are the color guards, majorettes and drum majors, all in the person of you. As you strut, you follow the guidance of your God, Who is the conductor of your soul, and He supplies and refuels the strength to strut with confidence. For He will never lead you where His hand cannot protect you. He will never take you where His grace cannot cover you and He will never guide you where His love cannot sustain you.

It goes without saying that you have been given the strength to strut, but what exactly are you strutting? You are strutting what has been given to you. However, in order to strut your stuff, you must know who you are. How can you strut what you do not know? It is impossible to strut that of which you are unaware that you possess. So, do you know who you are? Do you know what makes you tick? Do you know how to strum the strings of your inner self? What motivates you? What is it about you that's worth strutting? What do you possess that is worth others taking note and wanting to emulate?

You are strutting or showcasing your remarkable self and all that comes with who you are. However, your showcase isn't about entertainment purposes or for show. It is about bringing your best to the forefront at all times. It is about being ready and being on point. It is being ready to give an answer and to back up your words with positive action. It requires that you be equipped and prepared for the unprepared. For truth be told, when we are blessed to greet a new day, that is our wake up call to step up and to step out. In other words, your stage being set occurs when your feet hit the floor, the true runway of life. Your presentation started before you entered the boardroom. Your lecture was heard before you approached the mic. You are on display and must be runway ready before the open call. Forget the cameras clicking or the paparazzi parading, for whatever thoughts that you have of yourself will make an appearance and speak on your behalf, simply by your presence.

If, when you enter whatever arena, boardroom, store, lecture hall, or regardless of what door or threshold you cross, if your shoulders are slumped, feet slowly shuffling, face scowled, eyebrows knotted in representation for your stomach, you have already been defeated. It's written all over your face and body language. Yet you control your body. You control its' actions and reactions and regardless of the situation, you must enter the stage of life with the confidence of lessons that you have learned of yourself, the willingness to always improve and the promise to always be better.

Once you're able to hone in on who you are and the

remarkability of yourself, for the betterment of yourself and the servitude of others, you must decide how you're going to move from crawling, to walking and even strutting. Therefore, movement is vital and necessary for strutting purposes. For without it, you are simply standing still. Standing still too long opens the door for stagnation and to linger in stillness places a pause in your progress.

Of course, there are times when during your strut, life will require that you stop and stand, for the opportunity to take a snapshot of the scenery, to regroup, to assist another in the continuance of their strut, or to even leave your mark letting the world know that you were there, yet, be reminded that your goal is to keep it moving in life and that you have the strength required to continue on the journey.

However, there will be times, when life, uncontrolled as it can be, will require that you be still for more than a momentary pause. Life has a way of coming along unexpectedly and trying to replace your comma with a period. However, during your moment of stillness, your time should be spent learning more about you, sharing more of you with others and gradually getting back to the rhythm of you.

By choosing to strut, and all that it entails – the use of what you have received and the willingness to move to a better you, all the while enhancing others, the power that lies within you is unleashed and you are able to make and take steps towards the rediscovery of your best self. Then and only then can one go from walking, to taking steps that will lead to a strut as a result of your marching to the beat of your own drum.

In being able to strut, the confidence of your walk, your presence, location and the direction in which you are going requires that you possess something that is worth strutting.

Your refusal to strut your stuff denies you of the possibilities of your greatness and the power of the destiny that awaits. Your refusal to strut your stuff denies the world of your light and your opportunity to serve.

Strut your stuff, not only for yourself, but for all that you have encountered, have yet to encounter, as well as those that will be touched by the fact that you made the conscious decision to step where some feared to tread, to march where some refused to go and to walk along a path for others to follow.

So, how can we be ready, equipped and prepared, even for the unprepared? By taking the time to study and learn more of your most important commodity ~ you.

You have, you possess, you've been given the strength to strut. Now it's time for you to continue your personal journey of ST.Y.L.E. in the acceptance of who you are - a woman full of power, intensity, capability, endurance and passion.

STYLE

ON THE

INSIDE

'T'

TAILORED TREND

Tailored:

Fashioned or fitted

Trend:

To follow a general course

During our adolescent and young adult years, whether we are able to acknowledge it or not, we are trying to find our place in society. As we strive to figure out what works for us and what doesn't, mistakes are made and it's a trial and error type of journey. As we carve out our niche', we'll attempt various fashions until we find the right fit. Some attempts are of the subtle kind, while others scream and holler as they demand your attention, yet both are making a statement. They speak of our wanting to be seen and noticed for who we are. Not a carbon copy, but a never to be duplicated original.

There she was, one of my buddies, as well as one of the most popular girls on campus. So popular that she was crowned as the homecoming queen. She was a star athlete who was always impeccably and fashionably dressed. During our school days we would laugh, joke, encourage one another to study, and cheer each other on to be the best that we could be. One thing that was uniquely remarkable about my homie was her quest to make her own mark, to be unlike anyone else and to do something that spoke of her bubbly personality, as well as her eye for fashion. In knowing her, only she could've come up with the brilliant idea to polish her fingernails with one base color and placing a different color on top in various designs. I had never seen anything like it. Mind you, this was before nail salons had an inkling of enhancing nails. My homie took great pride in sporting stripes, wavy lines, or polka dots, being sure that each color coincided with her clothes, even if it meant that she had to change her fingernail polish every day. The key was the fashion statement being made.

She became known for this wacky, fashionable, one-of-a-kind designs and even when other people tried to copy her idea for themselves, it wasn't quite as snazzy because the idea originated with her. With her encouragement, I too, tried to paint my fingernails, but found that it wasn't for me. It wasn't that I didn't like her fashion choice. I actually appreciated and admired her fashion statement, but the upkeep of polished nails was never my thing, but for her, it was a perfect fit that enhanced her clothing style and personality. It was her Tailored Trend.

Everything doesn't work for everyone nor is everything meant for everyone.

A Tailored Trend coincides with the knowledge of what works for you and what doesn't – when to be aggressive, when to take low. It consists of being aware of the right opportunity to push the envelope on fashion or those moments that call for you to take a ride on the conservative side. When you follow your Tailored Trend, you are making wise decisions as to what fits your body, mind, soul and spirit and being aware of what doesn't. It's knowing when to unleash that pop of color to brighten the gloomiest of days or knowing that there are some days when that splash of color should be reserved for natures right. Whatever you decide, your tailored trends speak for you and serve as an example for others to follow. It's what you're sure of about yourself. It consists of the confidence in who you are, what you bring to the table and how to execute your gifts and talents to their full potential. Yet it is done without seeking the spotlight, though it is sure to follow your every move.

Knowing what works for you, as well as what does not,

goes beyond any fashion sense and requires that you have a plan in place that is tailored specifically for your needs, goals, desires and dreams. Your Tailored Trend takes the inner woman and your personality to the next level, to a point where others will not only see and hear you but will also wish to emulate what they have witnessed in you. No matter how hard someone may try, you are and always will be the one-of-a-kind original.

Just as with fashion, when it comes to your Tailored Trend, you must know your body type - the way a certain type of fabric clings or flows across your skin and accentuates each curve. It is important to recognize whether adding this or that would be too much or if it speaks of the undeniable style of you. When what you wear is worn well, with taste, class, funk, sophistication or sass, your entrance into any room will cause its' occupants to stand still, take note and want to duplicate the style that can only come from you and you alone. Your Tailored Trend speaks of what fits and works well for you today and tomorrow. The Tailored Trend, your plan, fits like a fine tailored suit because it was designed for you.

Your execution will draw others to seek to learn more of your ability to succeed. However, remember your journey is about more than who you are and the greatness that you possess for as your plan continues to unfold, you will become a catalyst for others to tap into the remarkability of who they are meant to be. Yet, try as they may, no one will ever be able to do what you do in the manner that you choose. Therefore, on your part, there is never the fear of duplication or a carbon copy rerun for the Divine Tailor has designed the creation of you. He has clothed and guides your greatness which leads to a positive on those around you. You have been blessed with a tailored made gift and talent that was designed to accentuate every curve of your character, to poise your personality and to increase your intellect.

In order for you to tap into and to seize your Tailored Trend, one must first own that they have been given and instilled with a talent and gift.

Everyone has been blessed with gifts and talents. Some of us have been blessed with the same gift, but your Tailored Trend propels you to add your unique way of bringing what has been instilled to the forefront. In other words, no one can do what you do, the way that you can do what you do.

You may consider yourself to be a gifted teacher. Within this universe, there are millions of teachers. So, you must ask yourself, what is it about your teaching style that causes you to stand out amongst the many? What is it about your strut, while teaching, that ignites a fire within your students, enabling them to actually enjoy learning rather than viewing education as an unnecessary need? What rhythm does your strut generate for your colleagues to want to emulate, imitate and even investigate its' origin in order to infuse it into their own curriculum? Your students, colleagues and those that you encounter are seeing a glimpse of your Tailored Trend and its' origin comes from a power greater than that of yourself. The Creator, your Divine Tailor, instilled an undeniable uniqueness within you upon your creation.

What is it about you that will cause them to desperately seek after your Tailored Trend, over and over again, as if what you possess is the very air that they breathe. What is your gift and your talent that when used, changes the world for the better? What is it that lies inside of you and that was given to you that adds color to an already designed flower or even shines brighter than a noon day sun?

What is a gift? A gift is something voluntarily transferred by one person to another without compensation. Our gift originated with the Creator, and He decided what would be given and to whom it would be given. The Creator does not seek payment, only our commitment to use what has been given for His glory and honor.

What is a talent? A talent is the natural ability of a person. Just as with your gift, it was instilled by your Creator and by choosing to use your talent, you are acknowledging what has been given and from whom it was given.

Your gift and talent were given to make the world better and to enhance the lives of all that you encounter during your journey. Imagine how marvelously wonderful this world would be if each individual lived in accordance with our gifts and talents. Gone would be the reason to fight. The rumors of wars would cease. Poverty, abuse, hatred, jealousy or envy would no longer exist, for each one would be so entrenched with giving that no one would compete in getting, if only to help, aid and assist the next person.

Now, ask yourself, have you been using what you've been given or have you made the decision to keep it on lockdown? If you've chosen to hinder the progress of your strut as it coincides with your Tailored Trend, it could be based on the fear that you will fail, the fear that others will laugh or the fear of unleashing the greatness that lies in you because of disapproval. What's the common denominator? Fear. F.E.A.R. - False Evidence Appearing Real. The failure and the laughter are false because they are based on an unreliable source. Even if you failed yesterday, that is not the conclusion of who you are and what you will accomplish on tomorrow. Failure is never final. If you stumbled yesterday, today, use it as a springboard for the victory that awaits. If you tripped during your strut and exhibition of your Tailored Trend, know that the runway continues and awaits your next step. If yesterday's laughter at your expense continues to echo in your ears, turn their laughter into your joy by refusing to continue to serve as the jester, for today you are the victor. Should someone disapprove of your greatness, that should never have a bearing on the approval of yourself for they had absolutely nothing to do with your creation or the completion of your being. They cannot supply the strength that fuels your strut or the Tailored Trend that undeniably speaks of who you are – remarkable and phenomenal. To internalize the narrow-minded opinion of another simply hinders the execution of your Tailored Trend. To heed their words encourages you to 'hide it under a bushel' which impedes the progress towards your glorious destiny and the opportunity for the world to be a better place by seeing your remarkable Tailored Trend.

The desired goal of your Tailored Trend is that the world will see it. hear it, feel it and be touched by it. Therefore, in exploring and discovering your Tailored Trend, there must be a definitive plan that will cause you to do more than simply exist, but one that will catapult you to a higher level. Your plan must be as specific as possible in order to cover every aspect of your desired conclusion, which calls for your being prepared for the unforeseen and the unexpected.

Whatever your needs, goals, desires and dreams, in order to achieve them it requires that you dig deep within your heart and soul, without fear. Therefore, be bold and fearless in your quest. Remember, this is your call to arms. This is the wake-up alarm for your Tailored Trend, which coincides with your strut.

So, ask yourself the following questions, what do you believe are your gifts and talents?

What do you plan to accomplish during your time spent on earth by using your gifts and talents?

How will your accomplishments serve others and make this world a better place?

Where exactly do you want to go and what exactly do you want to do?

How do you intend to execute your plan?

What sacrifices must be made in order to reach each level of achievement?

These are questions that can only be answered by you,

for to be tailored speaks of a fit that was created, designed and given solely to you.

However, consider and give special attention to the importance of creating the HEM that's necessary, which will bring about the ownership of your STYLE and bring you closer to the overall possession of your Tailored Trend:

- ❖ <u>H</u>onesty
- ❖ <u>E</u>limination & Incorporation
- ❖ <u>M</u>onitor

First, let's look at what it means to be honest, specifically with oneself. If each of us were to take a good look at ourselves, we would find areas within our lives that are worthy of applause and others that are areas of improvement. No one has cornered the market on perfection, and guess what, no one ever will. However, it is important that we look at ourselves for who we are, not how others perceive us to be, but for our true authentic selves. We should be able to stare at our reflection, naked of all our titles, categorical placements or even racial biases for regardless of the name plate on your office door, social status and the focus of the color of your skin, those things don't define who you are. You must look at who you are with appreciation for what has already been accomplished and knowing that the best is yet to come. If there are areas that yearn for improvement, and there are, call them for what they are and be dedicated to making the change. Is the ability to change beyond your reach? Never. Whatever area yearns for improvement can be accomplished as long as you are willing to make the effort to do so. Of course, change can be difficult, but in the end, you will be better for doing so and it will be worth it.

Second, the ability to eliminate those things from your life that will hinder you from reaching your goal. These could be negative habits, such as procrastination or doubt, but these eliminations go beyond what lies within you and it reaches those with whom you've surrounded yourself. Everyone that stands or sits next to you, or anyone that walks beside you or behind you, or whoever parts their lips to speak to you may not be for you. Based on where you are trying to go and the Tailored Trend that you offer, they may believe that they are serving as a means of support, when, in reality, they may be roadblocks towards progress. You've already been honest with yourself, now it's time to carefully study those that surround you. If they are not cheering you on, encouraging you, offering advice with your best interest at heart, being lovingly honest and even able to deliver a comforting push or nudge and willing to walk the mile, jump over hurdles and potholes with you, then perhaps they are hindering as opposed to helping. Yet be careful, for the elimination of such is a delicate process. Some will need to be kept at bay with a long handled spoon, while others may need to be placed in a category of negativity. By holding on to those who are unable to have your back for whatever reason, you have made a decision to carry and shoulder unnecessary weight and you're receiving what you've accepted. It's time for you to subtract, in order to add. It's time for you to trim the fat and build up your muscle. Don't tell yourself that 'this isn't personal' or that 'it's only business' for that's the furthest thing from the truth. It is personal because it's about the business of being you.

During your quest, many will offer words of advice and

guidance and it may come from those who have yet to tap into their Tailored Trend. Yet, you must be able to filter which is essential for your specific goal.

Your responsibility is to forever be gracious and willing to serve, while at the same time being cautious in knowing who is for you and who is against you. For those who appear to be against you, pray for them, for you realize that they are unable to appreciate your Tailored Trend for they have yet to even recognize their ability to possess their own. For those who are with you, hold them ever so close for they are rare jewels to be appreciated and they will assist in your growth.

It is just as important that you incorporate as you eliminate for you never want to find yourself being without. In order to incorporate and add to your life, ask yourself the following questions - how far do you want to go and what will you need in order to get there? This may take you beyond the boundaries from which you have found security. Adding will stretch, push and break the normalcy of which you've become accustomed and that, in itself can be overwhelming, however, your Tailored Trend demands that you step out on faith in order to go where your feet have feared to tread. It will call your courage to the carpet but this is your 'do or die' moment. What are you waiting for? Take the leap of faith and allow yourself to settle into your strut of faith while your STYLE becomes a powerful force to be reckoned with for the world is waiting to embrace your Tailored Trend.

For your Tailored Trend to be as effective as possible, it will require that you carefully monitor each aspect of your plan. It may call for the sacrifice of certain things, but it will be for your good. The one thing that must be monitored on a consistent basis is your time.

Though every person possesses their own gifts and talents, coupled with their goals, desires and dreams, every day we receive an identical and undeniable gift – TIME. Within each day, each individual receives the same twenty-hours as the next individual. The difference is choosing and making moves towards how one will use those fourteen hundred and forty minutes. Each minute was designed with you in mind and you must decide what you're going to accomplish with the gift of time that you've received.

Time cannot be wasted. Each of your eighty-six thousand and four hundred seconds should be filled with the abundance of who you are. You must live with the refusal of dwelling in the second that just expired or the anxiety of the one about to arrive. Simply live within the moment, drinking it in to the fullest, for as quickly as it arrives, so shall it depart.

Each day, you will have to set aside and carve out time that must be devoted to reaching your goal. The more time you give and the more urgent the need for you to make progress, the more time you will sacrifice for you. After a while, you will find that reaching your goal will become so essential and such a part of you, that you will eat, sleep and breathe your Tailored Trend. It will ooze from within the reservoirs of your soul through your pores and into the atmosphere. Believe me, the time spent in perfecting your Tailored Trend will not be wasted time, but will lead to worthiness. Soon, what began as a sacrifice of time will become a welcomed commitment towards the unveiling of your Tailored Trend.

With the realization that you must be honest with

yourself, eliminate those things that will cause a distraction or a hindrance. Have the courage to incorporate those things that are necessary to reaching your goal. Monitor every action and moment because time is not necessarily on your side.

I ask again, what do you want to accomplish? What do you want to do? Make your list. As a matter of fact, do it right now. Make the time to take an excursion into your mind and write these things down. No one can do this for you, this is your responsibility. Make a three tiered list. First, write down your immediate goals. These are goals that you are dedicated and committed to tackle right now. This column should consist of goals that are within your reach at this very moment. Second, make a column for your future goals. Determine the detailed timing and planning that you will need in order to execute and reach this goal. Detailed planning may consist of making a strategy that will include financial budgeting, creating a time line, contacting certain individuals, developing relationships with those that can assist with your implementation, as well as the marketing tools that you may want to use, just to name a few. Your last column should keep things light and fun, and serve as your reach-beyond-the-moon goals. If you'd like to see your name in lights on Broadway, write it down. If you're wanting to be listed as one of the world's top financial earners, write it down. If you want to receive the highest journalism award, put your pen in hand and write it down. If your beyond-the-moon moment is witnessing your Tailored Trend on a billboard sign or simply having a web site, record it. The skies the limit!

Why these lists? You have to be able to see it in order to achieve it. Write down everything that you want to do, each goal, every desire, every want and need. However, keep in mind that this list should consist of those things that will enhance who you are, enable you to make moves of improvement, and energize you to journey into unchartered territory. Don't waste time filling your life with useless tasks that will not serve to improve your present person or anyone else, therefore causing you to run the danger of being listed as an endangered species. Above all, hold yourself accountable for the completion with the refusal of making excuses.

Make your mark with the Tailored Trend that was

designed, fashioned and given solely to you by serving others which will lead and lend the world to your STYLE.

STYLE

ON THE

INSIDE

'Y'

YOUTHFUL ENERGY

Youthful:

Having or showing the freshness or energy of someone
who is young

Energy:

The physical or mental strength that allows you to do
things

As a child, it seemed as if I never tired. I would rip and run up and down the streets of Philly without a care in the world, never giving any thought to the fact that as one second came my way, another had just expired. I recall waking up on summer mornings with the bright sun streaming through the window panes of our ghetto home and jumping out of the bed, only to be assaulted by my mother with a broom and dust pan in hand. She would actually expect me to sweep the front concrete steps of our little home, along with the few cemented squares that belonged to our small plot of the sidewalk. In my mind, I'm thinking, surely, she has to realize that this menial household labor was slicing into my cool. After all, with all of the dirt and grime, who would really notice a freshly swept part of the sidewalk amongst the many miles of this concrete jungle. After all, some passerby would soon litter it with an empty potato chip bag, the amber glow of a smoked cigarette or worse. Yet, I grudgingly did it with quickness, because I knew that as soon as I was finished, I could go about my youthful activities. I would run upstairs, get cleaned up, make up my bed, grab my bike and fly over the steps that had already been littered because someone didn't know and probably didn't care that I had just swept them. These were my days of yesteryear, full of fun and power-packed with energetic activities to last from sun-up to sundown. Bike riding, skateboarding, basketball, playing tops in the middle of the street, numerous trips to the corner store or the water ice stand, sitting on the stoop with friends, laughing about ghetto life, or jumping on the subway for a trip to center city, only to return home just to do it all over again. Then of course, time was always set aside to go to the playground and watch the shirtless sweaty brothas run up and down the basketball court, until a fight ensued, and then it was back to a seat on the front steps that I had swept hours ago that was now free from the litter I had seen earlier, probably picked up by my mother. Even though she took take pride in her small plot of concrete ghetto soil, no matter how much she made me sweep or if she did it on her own, it was littered by an uncaring passerby or those of my friends. Throughout the day, my energy never waned. It remained so high that my appetite for a hot dinner, that required me to actually sit down for its' consumption, was usually vetoed for something of which I could partake while on the go in order to keep it moving. They weren't the healthiest choices, but I, nor my friends gave any thought to the caloric count, the salt intake or the carbs, as we threw down on now-and-laters, Swedish fish, chico sticks or a mustard pretzel, which was willingly shared with my cohorts. Even as the sun slowly set behind the horizon, I never tired. During the darkness of night is when the fun really began. The only ones thinking of jumping in the bed were those who couldn't hang. In the darkness, we paraded up and down the streets, swapped stoop for stoop, watched kids pop firecrackers, chased lightning bugs, stomped roaches (of course, I was too cute for that and I wasn't about to dirty up my white tennis shoes with the remains of some bug. Truth be told I was terrified of them), and we laughed until the whee hours of the morning. Those were the days of youthful energy. While time ticked away, life was carefree and the hustle and bustle was nothing more than a skip around the block.

These days, I'm still considered as one who has a lot of energy, however, today, I can feel the effects of aging and I am aware that those bike riding, hide-and-go-seek, non-stop rolling days, are not as they used to be.

Many a time, 'the spirit is willing, but the flesh is weak'. Honestly, I can't hang like I used to. Each day there seems to be a new ache, a newly heard pop of the joints, the need for stronger reading glasses and I'm becoming more familiar with 'arthur' and 'itis'.

There are some things in life that are beyond our control. One of those things is our age. We cannot turn back the hands of time, nor can we fast forward to a desired year. Upon our birth, we simply have to roll along with the tick tock of the clock and each year that we are blessed to see.

It's not until one has age on them, some mileage and responsibilities, that we sometimes long for those days of youthfulness and energy. Oftentimes, those are the days where we wasted more time, perhaps doing nothing. However, there's a trade-off, for along with age, comes wisdom. As we experience life, we learn more about life, ourselves and others. Yet, wouldn't it be great if there was a way to bottle that youthful energy that we once possessed and take a sip of it from time to time. If possible, it would serve as a fuel that would cause us to be as non-stop as the Energizer Bunny, who keeps going and going and going.

Reality reminds us that a magic potion doesn't exist. You could sip on every concoction or caffeine laced drink ever manufactured, in hopes of getting that big energetic boost but eventually the buzz will wear off.

You could even take it to a level of danger where you're popping pills to keep you going, but after a while, the energy will wain and the high will come down.

Here's the good news...though we are unable to control the clock, we have complete control of our attitude and our perspective during the age in which we find ourselves. The fountain of youth resides within each of us. Unfortunately, for some, the well has run dry as the soil from which the core of their inner being resides has become parched and cracked. The reason for the drought is based on the negative, narrow-minded and self-absorbing attitude that some have embraced and even guarded within their spirits.

How can we regain that youthful energy? Is it possible to find water in a desert where our dehydrated spirits have lived and, perhaps even become comfortable? The answer is a resounding yes! It's time to tap back into the youthful energy and the fountain of youth that we possess, therefore, unleashing a continuous wave that will nourish our souls, drench our spirits and wash away the cobwebs of complacency that have clouded our judgments and perceptions of who we are.

First let us examine our society. There are numerous commercials and advertisements that speak of the perfect potion, lotion or notion to erase those age lines, ages spots and shades of grey. Millions of dollars are spent on procedures to tuck, hide or cover those areas of the body that have given way to gravity, expanded with elasticity or even need to be tightened or uplifted, with the hopes of bringing about the former days of our youth. For some, it's as if they strive to surpass the pace of a clock that will never lose in the race of life.

Stories have been told of the search for the fountain of youth, but the spring of its' water resides within the reservoirs of our very souls. However, its' flow comes from the source of our minds.

Unfortunately, as we encounter life's stuff, some of us have allowed our encounters to send us on an excursion of denial that leads to a drought and famine of our spirits. With each refusal of the enjoyment of life and accepting it for the betterment and rediscovery of who we are meant to be, the ground of our souls becomes parched, cracked, and yearns for the life quenching waters of a healthy self-esteem and self- motivation.

True youthfulness resides in our minds for it is here that we find the embodiment and perception of ourselves. Our perceptions of who we see and our thoughts of who we are, give credence to the timeless saying that, "you're as young as you think you are' or that 'age is just a number'.

Of course this is not to say that age does not have its' place, for it does. A woman that has surpassed the half century milestone, will not or better yet, should not be found donning her body with the clothes that have been designed for a kindergartner and vice-versa. However, what we think of age, often shapes, forms and molds our ability to reach beyond the boundaries set for ourselves, simply on the basis of a double digit number.

When you're standing in front of a mirror, what do you think of you? It really isn't about whether or not you believe that your image coincides with your perception of your age. Who sets that standard anyway? Who has the authority to determine that someone looks good for their age? I'm not speaking of the attire, that's a choice, I'm speaking of the body and because each of us has our own, each body responds differently based on the experiences that we have and the way in which we care for what we've been given. When you look in the mirror, what causes you to tell yourself on one day that you're looking good and another day you're not? What happened to change your perception? Is this simply a thought process or a reality? King Solomon, spoken of as the wisest man in the world, tells us 'as a man (that includes woman for he is speaking of mankind) thinketh in his heart, so is he:' (Proverbs 23:7). Youthful energy starts in the mind. When you awake in the morning and as you go throughout your day, what you tell yourself about yourself is made manifest in how you walk, your communication with others, your choice of attire and your actions.

The mind, body, soul and spirit long for the spring of our fountain of youth to burst forth as a geyser that will nourish every fiber of our being. With each embrace of ourselves, the geyser will reach heights that will expand the boundaries of who we are and what we are able to attain.

Just as youthful energy begins in our thought processes, it is also important to realize that these thoughts of ourselves will manifest itself through our actions. Therefore, our wanting to be youthful and to remain youthful begins with the promise to take care of ourselves, for ourselves.

In order to obtain and remain in a state of youthful energy, calls for us to invest in the totality of who we are in taking care of and feeding our minds, body, soul and spirit. It is necessary to nourish every aspect in order to strengthen the strut which is tied to the tailored trend.

The feeding process begins with the mind, not the brain, for there's a difference. The brain is the organ that's responsible for our bodily functions. The mind is the ability to think, sense and process information. The mind is that part where our understanding takes place. Your brain coincides with the location of your body, whereas your mind can be focused on something that's on the other side of town. Which gives way to obtaining and continuing the concept of Youthful Energy by realizing the importance of Feeding the Mind.

My respected elders have impressed upon me a very simple principle when it comes to our minds, 'garbage in ~ garbage out'. If we fill our minds with negativity and if we choose to absorb and co-sign on those things that encourage a mindset of pessimism, then we will soon begin to act upon the dirt and grime that has infiltrated the cobwebs of our minds. In doing so, we are creating and fostering a breeding ground of hateration - hatred of self, hatred of others and hatred of all things positive and good.

Whatever we choose to feed our minds will determine the action to follow. Oftentimes, we are defeated by telling ourselves that we can't or that we won't, before our feet hit the floor. Too many times than not, the most gifted and talented psyche themselves out of being all that they can be by acting upon the fear that has been fostered in their minds. That fear then becomes an infection that grows into what can be categorized as a terminal illness and if left untreated it will overpower the mind. However, the good news is that there is a cure. The antidote is to feed the mind, those nutrients that are essential for healing and long lasting health. The antidote will consist of a regimen that must be consistent in order to do away with years of the negative stereotypes, the hateful words, the harmful actions and the degrading misconceptions that were ingested over the course of a lifetime. This is what has formed and shaped your perspective of yourself. Instead of focusing on those things, challenge your mind to think on the nutrients provided in a letter written to a church in Philippi. The writer encourages that whenever a damaging, degrading, or destructive thought tries to consume our minds, to think on things are true. Focus on things that are honest. Allow thoughts that are just, pure, lovely, and of good report to permeate and flow throughout the mind and it will cancel out those things that stand for the opposite (Philippians 4:8). This list of nutrients consists of mind blowing activities that will heal, help and harmonize every part of who you are, which includes the Feeding of our Bodies.

For years, the fashion industry has plastered pictures of waif, thin, emaciated women on covers of magazines and gracing the catwalk, that have shaped and molded the minds of the young and old. Over and over again, reports and pictures have surfaced of women that literally starve themselves, as their bodies are robbed of the nutrients needed to obtain a healthy body. Calories are counted, carbs are measured and serving sizes are studied for fear that in consuming one more cracker, one more slice of cheese, or one too many grapes, it will usher in those pesky fat cells, leading us down the road of obesity. Unfortunately, in other professions, women's bodies have been judged and exploited, in hopes of ensuring that they remain a certain size. Not only are there sizes, height and weight requirements for fashion models, but it even goes beyond the catwalk. For instance, for many years, the airline industry was criticized for checking the weight of their female flight attendants and in some cases, jobs were lost, lawsuits were filed and justice either prevailed or was denied.

Thankfully, the spotlight has shifted to the what is truly healthy and beautiful, but the fashion industry has a long way to go and many continue to suffer from the bias that is shown in hiring practices and circles of popularity, simply based on a woman's size and shape. Hear what I'm saying, it is important, very important that we eat healthy. It is essential that we are watchful as to what we eat. However, by all means, eat!

We should not over indulge, however in order to obtain Youthful Energy, we must eat. We must not live to eat, but rather eat to live. Carefully choose what ends up on your plate and blesses your palette. By eating, and making healthy choices, our bodies will respond to the food by absorbing the nourishment to make us better, not bigger. So, before indulging in a forkful of food, take a good look at what you've placed on your plate because whatever goes in will either be used as energy, to add to your youthfulness or it will turn to excess, which can impede your progress to the fulfillment of your STYLE.

Of course, there are those moments when our bodies crave those delectable, scrumptious, ooey, gooey treats. Of course, there are times when we want the flour-coated, deep-fried and finger-lickin' good bites of delight, of which we should be allowed to indulge from time to time. Partake in it but don't overdo it. After all, as hard as you're working, you deserve a treat from time to time. Therefore, feed your appetite, and after all is said and done, once you've pushed yourself away from the table and washed the dishes, allow your youthful side to break free. If running is too much, then jog. If not jogging, then walk but be sure to participate in some type of physical activity in order to stimulate your body. If you're engrossed in a mind tingling television show, instead of spending hours on the couch while consuming the calories, during each commercial break, if not every other, get up and walk. Not to refill an empty glass, unless it's water, or to replace the empty spot on your plate, but to get those arms swinging and your legs moving for just a few minutes. Stagnation of the body could lead to static within your five senses, creating an imbalance in your body's make up.

Look at it this way, your body is your temple, it's your house for which the upkeep and responsibility belongs to you. Even as we view super toned women, on the covers of magazines, that may or may not have been photo-shopped, admire the discipline but don't compare the process. Give kudos for the achievement but don't superimpose self-defeating thoughts of inability on your part. If you want to be better, then do better. What happens within your body, starts and ends with you. You are the sole proprietor of everything that is done within the house that you are building. A body that is youthful in its' outlook, youthful in its' in-look and youthful in its' energy.

Just as your Youthful Energy consists of the Feeding of your Mind and the Feeding of your Body, it can only be complete with the Feeding of your Spirit.

Your spirit is that part of you that speaks of your principle and personal force. It is the liveliness of you that longs to be fed on a consistent basis. To deny nourishment to your spirit denies you of the truth of who you are. To refuse sustenance to your spirit pushes you into a realm of settling for less than you were meant to be. Instead of allowing the freshness of your spirit to thrive, you are taking on counterfeit characteristics that cover and hide the existence that was meant for you. How can you possess a Youthful Energy when your spirit longs to be fed? How can the energy be of a long lasting quality when the feeding of your spirit is hit or miss? In order to ensure that your spirit is fed on a daily basis, one must search the spirit, satisfy the spirit and savor the spirit.

Searching your spirit determines those things that you're willing to tolerate and those that you are not. When we put up with what stifles our spirits, we run the danger of finding ourselves to close to that which can be detrimental. If you are confronted by something or someone that makes your spirit uneasy, yet you continue to further the allowance of that something or someone, then you are condoning its' presence within the boundaries of your inner self. Challenge and push yourself to the limits but be cautious in allowing someone else to do so, lest they rob and quench you of the Youthful Energy that longs to be free. If a robbery attempt is made in the case of your identity fraud, you will be found guilty in being the culprit and the criminal. You have committed assault on yourself. No one should be given access and permission to diminish the spirit that lies within, causing you to be untrue to yourself.

Those things and or persons that feed your spirit will bring you satisfaction. The satisfaction isn't found in your ego being pumped, but knowing that the best interest of your spirit is at heart. This group of individuals will serve as your cheerleaders and offering encouragement and submitting prayers on your behalf for they know of your goals, they are aware of your dynamic spirit and they understand that what affects you will also have a long lasting effect on them.

Be aware that as you grow and as your spirit leads you into exciting territories, it is important to remain true to who you are. Be flexible with what life brings, for it can change with the blowing of the wind and swell with the rushing tide. Therefore, the satisfaction of your spirit will call for you to never lose sight of the goal but to be at ease with whatever and whomever you encounter. With each goal that is met, the satisfaction of your spirit may challenge you to enlarge your territory and boundaries.

Whenever you have found something that tantalizes your senses, it's something that you want to continue to enjoy. You want to savor it for as long as possible. Your spirit must be savored, for to do so acknowledges that you are beyond content with the person of you. To savor your spirit is to celebrate your spirit. Not annually or based on a monumental event, but every day. Your celebration reminds you of your greatness and encourages you to soar beyond any limitations that anyone could set before you, as well as those that you once set for yourself. When you savor your spirit you aren't blindly ignoring your areas of improvement but you have chosen to focus on the power that lies within. You are attending a party where you are the guest of honor. Every day offers the opportunity for you to grow, to thrive and to serve someone else by feeding your spirit what is necessary to survive and remain in a celebratory state. This celebration of self will never exist without you - for it is you. You are the cream of the crop. You are the star that glitters in the atmosphere. You are the diamond in the ruff. Believe this, know this, allow your spirit to soar and savor the celebration that is you.

Your Youthful Energy must never be denied for whatever you do and wherever you go, your force is with you.

STYLE

ON THE

INSIDE

'L'

LUXURIOUS LIFESTYLE

Luxurious:

Very comfortable and expensive

Feeling or showing a desire for expensive things

Lifestyle:

A particular way of living

Many of the streets of Philadelphia, PA aka Philly, are filled with rowhomes. These are houses that have been constructed so that they are cemented together. Each wall is connected to the next. That means that if one house has roaches, those roaches are able to travel from one end of the block to another without having to go outside into the elements. The same can be said for rodents or any other creature that can fit between a crack or crawl into a hole. Some would even dare to say that this type of housing development can be categorized as a fire hazard for if one house catches fire, if not contained, the entire block can go up in smoke. It's these connected walls that also led to the hearing of fights, dishes being thrown, music being played, sex being had and the aroma of food.

Our home was the first house on our little block. While one wall was connected to that of our next door neighbor, the other wall served as a boundary for an alley, strewn with garbage that ranged from broken beer and whiskey bottles, to candy wrappers, and the discarded condoms that were used to wrap something else. All of this litter decorated the cracked concrete and silently spoke for the broken and cracked lives that were, perhaps looking for a better place to live, but had settled for the mediocrity of ghetto life.

Since our home was the first on the block, and because the homes were connected, if I wanted to, I could climb out of my parents' bedroom window and walk on the roof all the way to the corner without having to ever stop. I could even jump to the ground below, if careful and bold enough to do so. These were my surroundings. This was my world and my hood. Everyone in my world lived this way. Everyone within my circle of friends, and even those without, shared the same city, lived in the same vicinity, went from stoop to stoop, borrowed a cup of sugar or flour, walked down the same sidewalk and played in the same street. Even if it was on the other side of the city, it was the same, just a different street, with different numbers. Each city dweller had a small plot of concrete, perhaps a small patch of grass, an occasional tree or plot of bushes, and weeds that were bold enough to squeeze through the concrete and make an announcement that they existed, only to be trampled underfoot.

My elementary school, The Little Red School House,

lived up to its' name. It was a rectangular red building that was set within the confines of a tall chain-linked fence. Our school days were spent inside of one room, unless we were granted recess, which was nothing more than an adventure into our childhood game of imaginations, for there wasn't a playground or even a box of sand. Recess simply consisted of exiting the door of The Little Red School House and finding a concrete spot to run, play, jump or to sneak away from the sometimes, watchful gaze of the teachers tired assistant so that we could add to the graffiti that served as portraits of art.

Gang wars were running rampage throughout the city, of which school kids found their acceptance and the camaraderie that had long gone AWOL within the confines of their row homes. Fights were a daily occurrence and it was for this reason that my parents made the decision to pull me out of the public school system, away from the prison yard of the Little Red School House and sent me to a school that had not been touched or affected by ghetto laws and traditions.

It was here, more than an hour outside of my city, that I

witnessed that there was more than ghetto life. This new school boasted of lush, green fields for various outdoor sports, rolling hills, parking lots, a playground that looked like a potential paradise, and all of it was framed and surrounded by trees. The air even smelled fresher. The breeze seemed cooler. Gone were the chain-linked gates and the graffiti. Even the absence of concrete left me wondering if I was still in the same state. Within the classroom, I had my very own desk and chair and even though I was the only African-American girl in my class, my reason for feeling out of place was due to the unfamiliarity of my surroundings. Being in this new environment, I met people and made friends that actually lived in homes with lawns. Before, I had only seen such homes on the Brady Bunch, but these people were alive and in color. They were talking to me, eating beside me, and sharing my classroom. Before, to actually live in a home that had more than a patch of grass, plus a garage and even a pool was such a foreign concept. Our home was kept neat, tidy and clean by my mother, but in seeing that there was another way to live, my mind categorized the suburban homes as luxurious. It was my eyewitness account that stretched the boundaries of my imagination and gave way to reality. It caused me to do more than dream, but to reach and to push beyond the possibilities of my ghetto boundaries.

My perceptions of luxury were once again challenged as I began to model. To grace the catwalk where the price of an outfit went beyond the weekly or monthly salary of a minimum wage working individual told me that someone out there had the means whereby they could purchase that shirt, skirt or shoes or outfit without blinking an eye. Therefore, the change in my surroundings taught and showed me that the Luxurious Lifestyle was not only real, it was attainable.

For a homeless person a Luxurious Lifestyle could be a bed, even if that bed is encased in a jail cell. For another a Luxurious Lifestyle is a mansion, complete with servant quarters and a staff ready to wait on its' owner hand and foot. Yet, for another a Luxurious Lifestyle could simply be the well-being of the mind, the ability to pay bills, to eat a warm meal, to enjoy a night free of an abusive predator, freedom from fear or to have clean water. The definition of luxury is dependent upon encounters, experiences, as well as the lifestyle from which one has been born and where they would like to see themselves.

Regardless of the level of luxuriousness, the quest leads to a life that is willing to reach for what is better or what is best. The decision is yours. However, one cannot limit themselves based on what you've been conditioned by and what you have been conditioned to do.

Many of us have heard the phrase, 'when you know better, you do better', which lends itself to the belief that one is unable to do what they do not know. Even in witnessing what is considered better, the path to getting there requires knowing - knowing how, knowing when, knowing why and knowing the who's who.

The 'how' of luxury can only be obtained with an open mind. Of course educating oneself broadens the horizons of our possibilities, however, education alone, does not open the door. There are many who are educated, yet ignorant for they lack the wisdom that leads to the implementation of what they have come to know.

Knowing when to make that move and when to be still is crucial. If the door of opportunity opens, you must know when to walk beyond the threshold, instead of choosing to linger within the shadows that have become a comfortable security blanket. Too many have refused to take hold of the opportunity that awaits, hoping that another will make an announcement, when the blaring wake-up alarm beckons for them to move forward. On the flip, there are others who move too soon, when the atmosphere calls for one to be still and to wait. So, when would be the most advantageous time to make key moves? When the heart, the mind, and the spirit are on one accord, then more times than not, your 'when' moment has arrived.

The heart speaks of your emotions. Oftentimes, our emotions get the best of us and we get caught up too quickly. The mind is your thought process - the facts, figures and your knowledge of what stands before you. Your spirit is your conscience. It is your sixth sense. It tells you that this is a good fit for you or it brings caution to the forefront.

Knowing why is the understanding of your motivation. Why are you doing what you're doing? Why are you seeking what you're seeking? Are your movements based on a past pain, a solution to a problem, making provisions for a supply and demand, a unique idea, your passion, a whim that you are hoping will catch on or a combination of the aforementioned? This is a question that is imperative for it will lead you to your 'who'.

Another well-worn and well-used quote says, 'it's not what you know, it's who you know'. You could have the best laid plans and the best intentions, but if you are not hooked up with the proper 'who's who' then you may find yourself spinning your wheels. However, the 'who's who' deals with two different groups of people. The first group are those who will benefit from your plan. Who do you hope to serve, help, aid and reach? The second group of the 'who's who' will assist you to reach the first group. Who will help you to get where it is that you want to be? Who should be your 'surround sound system', in other words, who do you trust to give sound advice and who will help you to get to the next level?

Of course, one may ask, is enough ever enough? Is there ever a level of contentment? What happens when you finally reach that goal, buy that house, climb that mountain, jump over that hurdle, reach that level, graduate from that school, and the list goes on and on. Should we settle for where we find ourselves, once we arrive? Should we tell ourselves that this is it or that this is as high as we were meant to go?

For me, the answer is a resounding no. In the Gospel according to the Apostle John, the Savior tells us that He came 'that we might have life and to have it more abundantly' (John 10:10). As long as there is life, there is the opportunity for improvement. When we are open to life and all that it can bring, with the various experiences and encounters, we should always be in a state of learning and yearning. When our hearts and minds are open to the value of every person, we realize that we are able to learn, even from the smallest of children. When we allow ourselves to grasp all that life can offer, we teach ourselves to focus on the blessing of learning more of ourselves and those around us and in doing so, we are forever in a state of learning and yearning. Not yearning to do better, but to be better. Therefore, our experiences of life, our meetings and greetings should catapult us to a higher level when we are open and honest with who we are and our ability to be in a state of forever growing.

Just as it is important to understand the concept of how, when, why and who, in order to take advantage of a Luxurious Lifestyle, one must also do the following:

- ❖ Conquer Fears
- ❖ Consult Carefully
- ❖ Choose Wisely

Fear, as an acronym, stands for False Evidence Appearing Real. Conquering fears dismisses any apprehension of moving forward into what may be unchartered territory. Even though the direction that you are striving to go is unfamiliar, you have prepared for this moment and there is no need to fear. Once steps are taken, should the flame of fear become ignited with the danger of turning into a roaring inferno, your Strength to Strut should extinguish it immediately. It is also your Strength to Strut that will stand as a guard of security so that any future flames of fear will be denied the opportunity to ignite.

To consult carefully is tied in with the 'Who's Who'. Those that will assist in your journey to where you want to be will offer sound advice based on their expertise. However, be aware that what has worked for others, may not work for you. Therefore, consult more than one and once advice is offered and received, be sure to show gratitude for the time and expertise given. More than likely you will find a variety of opinions and advice. This variety of opinions should not be seen as a negative, but will grant you the opportunity to take what has been offered, and the time to search your heart, mind and spirit.

Choosing wisely is weighing the pros and cons of the advice which has been given based on where you want to be and where you want to go. Your decision must be made knowing that you have the Strength to Strut, that it will coincide with your Tailored Trend and that it will enhance your Youthful Energy. You may have to step out and try the suggestions given, but this is necessary in order to know what will be of benefit and what will not. This concept also gives way to the realization that if you have consulted carefully, then whatever direction you choose to follow, it will not be wasted time but either a learning experience for future endeavors or the correct choice.

As you begin to partake in your Luxurious Lifestyle, whether it entails your peace of mind, healthy choices such as increasing your water intake, a workout regimen, a change in sleeping habits that add to your Youthful Energy, meditation, or financial decisions that have served their purpose, remember to live. Enjoy your luxurious life. Don't compromise your values or swap your beliefs in order to achieve a position. Simply live knowing that as your life changes with each passing day, your idea of a Luxurious Lifestyle is within your reach. Continue to tap into the Strength that allows you to Strut, continue to make and leave tracks based on your Tailored Trends, and reach and explore the possibilities of your Youthful Energy. The continuance of these principles will afford you the opportunity to grasp your Luxurious Lifestyle.

STYL<u>E</u>

ON THE

INSIDE

'E'

EMBRACE YOUR

ESSENCE

Embrace:
The act of clasping another person in the arms;
the state of taking in or encircling

Your:
Of you or yourself

Essence:
The true nature of anything;
the defining property of something; center; core;
heart and soul

New York City – the Big Apple. A city described by Alicia Keyes as the "concrete jungle where dreams are made of..." I, along with millions of city dwellers, whisked through the streets. Though my footsteps were practically a slow jog, the pace couldn't keep up with the beating of my heart. My shoe bag was draped over one shoulder and my make-up bag in the other.

While standing at the corner, waiting for the red light to turn green, I took in my surroundings. I heard the honking horns and listened to the fire engine sirens in the distance, while a never ending stream of taxis threatened to run over any or every nationality of shopper, tourist, business man or woman, relocating sidewalk sleepers.   I allowed myself one more second to look up at the side by side skyscrapers, standing as soldiers in an unnamed war, that disappeared into the clouds above and then... 'SPLASH', the first raindrop smacked me in the middle of my forehead. The light turned green as I was caught up again into the wave of people moving quickly towards the shore of their destination. SPLASH! Another raindrop, heavier than the first, hit my head as I quickened my pace. I practically started to run, hoping to make it, trying to reach and wanting to be where I needed to go. I turned the corner on my heels, flying through the door just as the onslaught of torrential rain began to fall. It was as if the heavens opened and the sky cried tears of joy for me. The raindrops were descending in celebration for my being here. Of course, the rain was God's way of cleaning and saturating the earth, but on this day, I told myself that His creation was rejoicing with me for my invitation, acceptance and arrival to participate in the prestigious New York Fashion Week.

Here I stood in a room that can only be described as electrified. The current flowed from person to person as each served as their own transformer, unleashing a power of their own.

Here I stood, preparing for another fashion show, but, of course, this one was different. It had a different vibe, a higher level of intense excitement and an extreme busyness as models lined the walls, sat on the floor or huddled in corners. This was, after all, New York Fashion week – the sought after fashion arena for designers and models.

In the weeks prior to the fashion show, lanky, thin, tall

models stood in lines that wrapped around buildings, like a cattle-call, in order to be one of the lucky ones to grace the catwalk. I'm sure that the moment of hoping to be chosen left many a model experiencing nail-biting, stomach-churning minutes of anxiety that quickly faded as names were called. The favored few beamed with pride while those whose names were never trumpeted into the atmosphere walked away with discouragement and feelings of rejection.

Here I stood, never having to stand in a line or to be paraded in front of designers for their nod of approval for I had been invited to participate and to therefore, grace the catwalk with my signature strut. I was humbled, excited, anxious and energetic. Like the other models, I went from station to station, having make-up applied, hairstyles chosen, met with designers and tried on clothing for the last minute touches and nods of approval, all the while, waiting for the show to begin. The music was our cue. The thumping of the bass that flowed behind the runway grabbed us, wrapped itself around our bodies and we marched towards the curtain waiting for our individual opportunity to grace the catwalk in front of a crowd filled with fellow designers, guest celebrities, famous athletes and paparazzi. As I entered to walk, I never noticed the flash of cameras or even those who were seated on each side of the runway. There was no time to feel or take note, only to do. To do what I had been invited for – to strut. Unlike my first show, the jitters were gone and my nerves had intertwined with the beat of my heart, my spirit and my soul. My journey had allowed me to experience the joy of embracing my essence, causing me to expand my boundaries and excel in the comfort and acceptance of who I was, who I am and who I will become with each step from that moment and those to follow.

To Embrace Your Essence entails being about the business of you. It is the acceptance of the entity that is you, without apology, excuse or explanation. You have affirmed who you are with the acceptance of your greatness based on your ability. You have ceased to compare yourself with others for in doing so, it snuffs out the inner glow that was given to you and it also causes the other to be placed on a pedestal that was meant for you. You are hugging yourself. You are finally able to give yourself the encouragement that you are due and that you need in order to continue your signature Strength to Strut, to tweek or revitalize your Tailored Trend, to foster a youthful attitude that ushers in Youthful Energy and leads you to you Luxurious Lifestyle with passion and absent of regret or remorse.

To Embrace Your Essence calls for you to become fully involved in each Experience, urges you to Expand your boundaries and to Excel with every fiber of your being.

The Experience

Each step has led you to this moment. Every experience, every encounter, all of your movements, every action, each inhale and exhale and all of your spoken and unspoken words. It even encompasses the reach of your hands, the touch of your fingertips, the turn, shake or nod of your head, those things within your direct view and your periphery, all of it, everything has led you to this place in your life. It includes the highs and lows, mountains and valleys, sun kissed days or stormy nights, tears and laughter, backstabs and handshakes – everything that you have done, witnessed, felt, and heard has played a monumental force to the destination of today.

Some things may have appeared as a hindrance, when in reality, each experience was allowed to equal the totality of you. In doing so, you have been blessed with the opportunity of experiencing the essence of who you are without regret or remorse. Prior to your in-depth revelation, you were simply scratching the surface of your abilities, but now, the clouds of doubt, fear, procrastination, insecurity, sabotage and worthlessness have dissipated. Today you are able to stand on your own, to step on your own, to strut with an undeniable strength. Now you are ready to run, to soar, and to explore the possibilities that await. As each experience leads and gives way to another, you experience the phenomenon of you. Therefore, today, you will look upon, greet and welcome the person of you with gratitude of heart. You now possess a mind of determination, a body that is in tune with the purpose of creation, you hold an appreciative in spirit, and a soul that holds an eternal glow.

Expand:

As you embrace your experiences, it leads to your ability to Expand. Each experience has served as the fertilizer of your essence and now, growth is eminent. It is time to make the shift of your dreaming and daring to actually doing by increasing and enlarging the scope of your territory. It is time for you to break free and to move beyond the boundaries that were put in place by someone else and even yourself.

The challenge of your breakthrough and break-free moment urges that you make the shift from that in which you were comfortable. For in doing so, the challenge seeks to push you beyond where you've always been, what you've always done and those with whom you've surrounded yourself.

If the scenery looks the same or if it appears that you keep passing the same landmark, chances are it's because you've been going around in circles. Without a doubt, you were there for a reason and your time was well-spent as it has served as a place of learning and growth. However, as lessons have been learned and questions answered, there is no longer the need to continue spinning your wheels. Eventually, your laps around the track will turn into a trench and before you know it, you will become trapped. For the walls of the trench, that once seemed insurmountable will begin to serve as the mote that keeps you imprisoned from venturing into a world that awaits your arrival. And so, you must move. Your growth requires that you break free from the harness of your familiar surroundings. You must cross the line that was drawn in the sand and breach the boundaries for the benefit of your tomorrows.

Your failure to do so will lead to your being smothered, stifled and stagnant. Your refusal to step forward gives power to your fear rather than your faith. Your movement is necessary and your growth is imperative. Your expansion will not allow you to remain where you've been planted. For as you grow, you will stretch the space that you have occupied until it is no longer able to hold you, leading to the birth of life that has been waiting for you.

Your break-free and breakthrough moment may not be easy. You've become comfortable with the familiarity of your present surroundings even though it has become detrimental to your growth. It will call for you to step into unchartered waters, but this is a sink or swim decision. You will either drown in the murkiness of your constant treading or you will swim into the deep waters of desire where destiny awaits. The choice is yours. Yet keep in mind that every experience was given to lead to your expansion, not to hold you as a hostage. It is time to step.

Excel

Now it is time to live. You thought that you were living before, but I beg to differ. Hear me when I tell you that your Strength to Strut, Tailored Trends, Youthful Energy, Luxurious Lifestyle and Embracing Your Essence have awakened you, and now it's time to not only feed off of each experience and to grow, it's now time for you to soar. This is your moment to take off down the runway of life, to accelerate and take off to higher heights.

You are required to go beyond your bloom in order to reach your blossom. You had enough courage to break through the soil, to break the boundaries and shatter the handcuffs that were holding you hostage, but it's not enough. Breaking through is just the beginning. You want to be more than average and beyond mediocre, you want to surpass and exceed the recommended dose of who you are. Those who stepped to you, stepped by and stepped over you may have manufactured a dosage that you were willing to drink, but they are not aware of, responsible for nor are they able to comprehend nor control the gift that was given to you. Their concoction was never meant for you, it was a recipe of consumption meant for them and the longer you continue to sip and attempt to savor what was not meant for you, the more bitter it will become.

Now that you have been able tunnel through to see the sun, you will want to do more than observe its ?, you will want to feel the warmth that it brings. For you know that it will warm your soul and now you can e. by moving beyond your blossom and making the decision to bloom. To bloom calls for you to handle your business. It's the stamp of approval on yourself. As you Embrace Your Essence, your surroundings, and your associations of self and others will change, for you will be able to see the greatness of who you are and the ability that others can bring. Therefore, it is imperative that you surround yourself with others that are likeminded in striving to make and meet their goals, so choose carefully.

By hugging yourself or by Embracing Your Essence, your true character comes through, for you will find that not everyone will be able to handle the shimmer and shine of your STYLE. Yet, be aware that it is alright.

Not everyone is expected to be open to your glow.
Though you offer others the opportunity to do the same,
some may shy away from your shine. Some may cower
in the glow of your greatness. Be encouraged to know
that those who may excuse themselves for shade and
attempt to throw it your way were only meant to be there
for a temporary moment.

And for those who are chosen to occupy your inner
space, choose wisely. Other STYLE setters and STYLE
lovers will find their way to you as a means of support
and strength. Those chosen must be by invitation only
for this fellowship of friendship will increase your
momentum. Your strut will begin to pick up speed as it
matches the beat of your heart and Your passion. Those
that march with you, side by side, will serve as your
cheerleaders and your co-workers in the journey towards
the fulfillment of your goals. They are with you, not for
competition but to encourage you to Embrace your
Essence as you embrace your own. As you learn and
gain from one another, you will also grow with one
another. This will be your inner circle and those who
are willing to recognize the gift of your greatness as they
have embraced their own. Soon others standing on the

sidelines will wonder how they, too, can join in the strut of success. They will want to know what it takes to keep up with your pace, and while they are standing and cheering, hating or appreciating, you'll be doing.

Will the embrace ever get to the point where your momentum slows? There will be times when you will learn to cruise while basking in the glow of your light, but this is also a time for rejuvenation, renewal and refreshment. This is the opportunity to retreat in order to refuel and refine in order to remain relevant. You are soaring on the wings of your essence. You are gliding on the winds of determination. Here, you are given the opportunity to embrace the reflection of where you stand, and being made aware of the moment to, once again, move.

As you Embrace Your Essence, move with determination with the understanding that being about the business of you entails more than you. It's your power within that pushes, urges and encourages you to empower another, leading to your legacy. For you see, the business of you is about more than you. Your Strength to Strut, Tailored Trend, Youthful Energy,

Luxurious Lifestyle and Embracing Your Essence creates footprints of hope for others to follow. In the end, isn't that what life is truly all about? Saving and serving others. Your STYLE lends itself to another and offers them permission to exhibit their very own. Not to copy, imitate or duplicate, but to seek the personal purpose that was destined in the very beginning.

Questions and Thoughts for Consideration:

Experience: What experiences of yesterday have shaped your goals for today?

Expansion: What are you willing to sacrifice for your goals?

What is important to you?

Excel: As you gain momentum, identify one person that you are willing to mentor.

THE

CONCLUSION

Conclusion:

the end or finish

The truth of the matter is that when it comes to your STYLE, there is no conclusion, for it will never end. You will forever evolve, change, learn and grow and the absence of such is the beginning of extinction. Your STYLE will forever lend itself to another. It will reach and touch those long after you have ceased to breathe. Your STYLE will have a long-lasting effect on generations that have yet to be born, for we do not exist without touching the lives of others, positively or negatively.

It is my prayer that your STYLE will touch, cradle and reach the masses in a positive sense. It is my prayer that you will forever be granted the STRENTH to STRUT, dazzle the world with your TAILORED TREND, possess a YOUTHFUL ENERGY, lead a LUXURIOUS LIFESTYLE and EMBRACE YOUR ESSENCE.

I trust that you will do these things and so much more for you have been gifted with...

STYLE

ON THE

INSIDE.

Made in the USA
Columbia, SC
20 October 2017